My First Joke Book

ARCTURUS

ARCTURUS

This edition published in 2018 by Arcturus Publishing Limited
26/27 Bickels Yard, 151–153 Bermondsey Street,
London SE1 3HA

Illustrated by: Amanda Enright and Kasia Dudziuk
Additional images: Shutterstock
Text by: Paul Virr
Designed by: Trudi Webb
Edited by: Joe Harris and Sebastian Rydberg

ISBN: 978-1-78828-520-9
CH006111NT
Supplier 29, Date 0818, Print run 6801

Printed in China

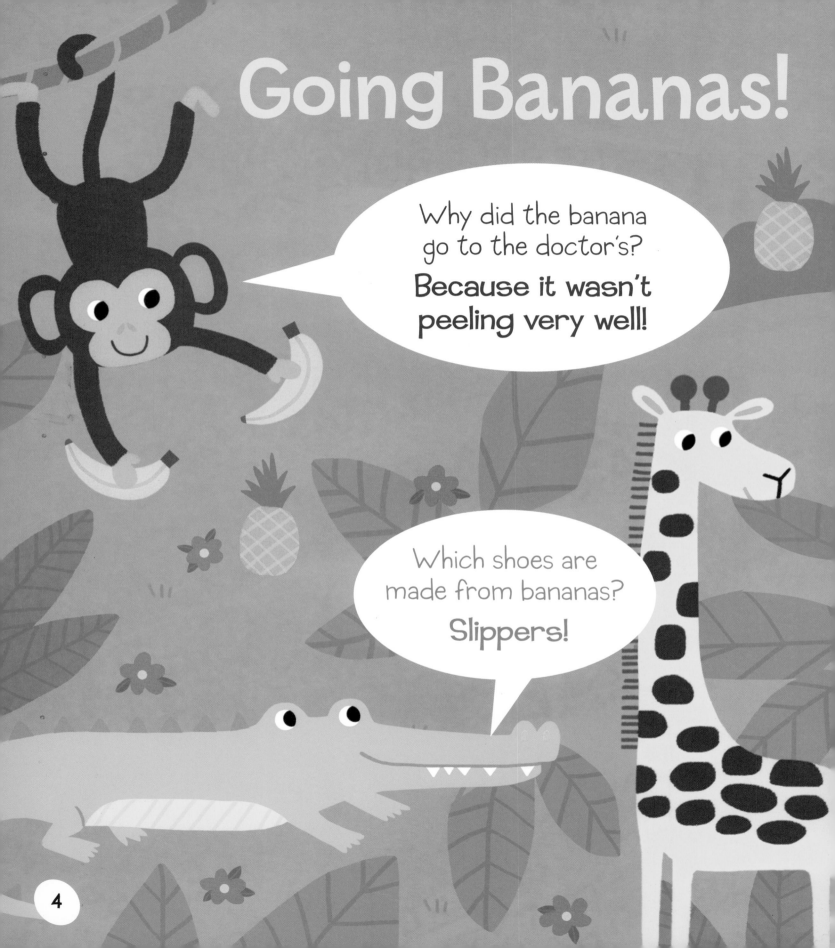

5

Fang-tastically Funny!

Why do vampires chew gum? Because they have bat breath!

What type of dog does a vampire have? A bloodhound!

Fairy-Tale Fun!

Why do dragons sleep during the day?
So they can fight knights!

Why is a fairy-tale king like a piece of wood?
Because he's a ruler!

9

Funny Bunnies!

What kind of story does a bunny like reading?
One with a hoppy ending!

What did the rabbit say to the carrot?
It's been nice gnawing you!

Snake School

What kind of snake is good at sums?
An adder!

What is a snake's best subject at school?
Hiss-tory!

Vampire School

What do vampires never have for lunch?
Steak!

Why did the vampire teacher go crazy?
His students drove him batty!

All at Sea!

What do you call a baby whale?
A little squirt!

Why did the shark blush?
It saw the ship's bottom!

Fast-Food Fun!

19

Going Batty!

What do vampire bats do when they meet up? **They just hang out!**

Why did the mean vampire have no friends? **Because he was a pain in the neck!**

23

An Apple a Day?

Why did the apple burst into tears?
Someone had hurt its peelings!

Which apple is like a Christmas tree?
A pine-apple!

27

What a Hoot!

29

Munching Monsters

Why are vampires always hungry? Because they eat necks to nothing!

What do monsters have for dessert? Ice scream!

Crazy Cats!

What do you call a young cat that becomes a doctor?
A first aid kit!
HOSPITAL
What do cats eat for breakfast?
Mice crispies!

33

A Pizza the Fun!

Waiter, do you think my pizza will be long?
No, I think it will be round!

Why did the student become a pizza chef?
He needed to make some dough!

Zany Zoo

What do penguins love to eat? Ice-burgers!

Why did the tiger follow the lion? He was a copycat!

Monster Party!

What do you call a vampire that's always hungry?
Snackula!

Which monster is always playing tricks on people?
Prank-enstein!

39

Dippy Dogs

Did you hear about the dog that could tell time?
It was a watchdog!

Why was the dog scratching after it went shopping?
It had been to a flea market!

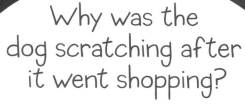

41

Mischievous Mice!

How do you make a mouse smile?
Ask it to say cheese!

Why are mice so tidy?
They always do the mouse-work.

45

Monsters on the Move

What car does Frankenstein drive?

A monster truck!

What do you call a witch with a broken broom?

A witch-hiker!

47

Silly Space Food

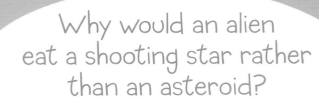
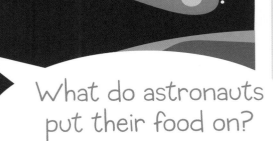

49

Totally Quackers!

What time does a duck wake up? **The quack of dawn!**

Where did the duck go when she was sick? **To the ducktor!**

Wacky Woodland!

Wacky Werewolves

Which monster can help you if you get lost? **A where-wolf!**

Did you know I used to be a werewolf? **I'm much better noooooooow!**

Fruity Fun!

57

Jokes Ahoy!

Why couldn't the pirates play cards? Because their captain was standing on the deck!

What do you call a pirate without an eye patch or a wooden leg? A beginner!

Hopping Mad!

61

Silly Spells

What do you call a nervous witch?
A twitch!

Did you hear about the twin witches?
Nobody knew which witch was which!

Dizzy Drinks!

What soft drink
do frogs like?
Croak-a-cola.

How does a
penguin drink juice?
Out of a beak-er!

Out of This World Jokes!

Where do you find black holes?
In black socks!

What did the alien say to the gardener?
Take me to your weeder!

Jumbo Jokes

Which game should you never play with an elephant?

Squash!

Why are elephants so wrinkly?

Have you ever tried to iron an elephant?

68

What do you get if you cross elephants with fish?
Swimming trunks!
What do you call the king of the giraffes?
Your high-ness!

Monstrously Funny!

What kind of sandwich do sea monsters like the best?
Sub sandwiches!

How do you get rid of smelly monsters?
With scare freshener!

71

Soupy Loopy!

Waiter, why is the tablecloth all wet?
You ordered leek soup!
Waiter, just what is this fly doing in my soup?
The backstroke, I think!

Ridiculous Robots!

What do you call a robot that loves swimming?
"Rusty!"

How can you get a robot to come to your birthday party?
Send it a tin-vitation!

Un-bear-ably Funny!

What do you call bears with no ears?
Bees!

What kind of gym shoes do bears wear?
They don't wear any. They go bear-foot!

77

Sick Monster Jokes

How do you know when a vampire has caught a cold?
He keeps coffin!

Did you hear about the witch who caught a cold?
The doctor told her to stay in bed for a spell.

79

Silly Sandwiches!

Fairyland Funnies!

What do you call a fairy that needs a bath? **Stinkerbell!**

Why did the naughty fairy have to leave school? **She was ex-spelled!**

Playful Penguins

What do you call a penguin in the desert?

Lost!

Why do penguins carry fish in their beaks?

Because they don't have any pockets!

Scary Sports Day

Who won the vampires' running race?
It was a draw-they all finished neck and neck!

Which sport does a giant, big-footed monster play?
Squash!

A Fridge Full of Fun!

Why did the tomato turn red? **It saw the salad dressing!**

Why was the beanpod always running around? **He was full of beans!**

89

What's the Buzz?

What flies through the air and goes "zzub, zzub"?

A bee flying backward!

How do bees get to school?

They catch the school buzz!

Why do bees have sticky hair?
They use honeycombs!

What are the cleverest insects?
Spelling bees!

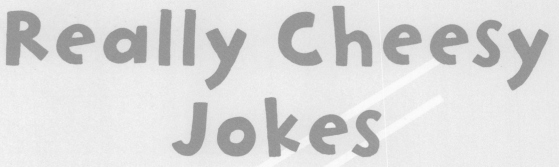

Really Cheesy Jokes

It's Snow Joke!

What do you get if you cross the Abominable Snowman with a crocodile?
Frostbite!

How does the Abominable Snowman relax?
He just chills out!

What's on top of the
Abominable Snowman's bed?
A blanket of snow!

How does the Abominable
Snowman score a goal?
With a snowball!

Loony Moon!

Why did the cow blast off into space?
She wanted to see the Moooooooon!

What do astronauts like to read?
Comet books!

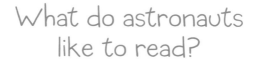